The Galleons

ALSO BY RICK BAROT

The Galleons

poems by

Rick Barot

MILKWEED EDITIONS

Published 2020 by Milkweed Editions
Printed in the United States of America
Cover design by Mary Austin Speaker
Cover art by Alfredo and Isabel Aquilizan
20 21 22 23 24   5 4 3 2 1
First Edition

Milkweed Editions, an independent nonprofit publisher, gratefully acknowledges sustaining support from the Alan B. Slifka Foundation and its president, Riva Ariella Ritvo-Slifka; the Ballard Spahr Foundation; *Copper Nickel*; the Jerome Foundation; the McKnight Foundation; the National Endowment for the Arts; the National Poetry Series; the Target Foundation; and other generous contributions from foundations, corporations, and individuals. Also, this activity is made possible by the voters of Minnesota through a Minnesota State Arts Board Operating Support grant, thanks to a legislative appropriation from the arts and cultural heritage fund. For a full listing of Milkweed Editions supporters, please visit milkweed.org.

Library of Congress Cataloging-in-Publication Data

Names: Barot, Rick, 1969- author.
Title: The galleons : poems / Rick Barot.
Description: First edition. | Minneapolis, Minnesota : Milkweed Editions, 2020.
Identifiers: LCCN 2019022928 (print) | LCCN 2019022929 (ebook) | ISBN 9781571315236 (paperback ; acid-free paper) | ISBN 9781571317278 (ebook)
Classification: LCC PS3602.A835 A6 2020 (print) | LCC PS3602.A835 (ebook)
 | DDC 811/.6--dc23
LC record available at https://lccn.loc.gov/2019022928
LC ebook record available at https://lccn.loc.gov/2019022929

Milkweed Editions is committed to ecological stewardship. We strive to align our book production practices with this principle, and to reduce the impact of our operations in the environment. We are a member of the Green Press Initiative, a nonprofit coalition of publishers, manufacturers, and authors working to protect the world's endangered forests and conserve natural resources. *The Galleons* was printed on acid-free 30% postconsumer-waste paper by Versa Press.

for my mother and father

CONTENTS

The Galleons

THE GRASSHOPPER AND THE CRICKET

The poetry of earth is a ninety-year-old woman
in front of a slot machine in a casino in California.

She is wearing a gray dress, her sharp red lipstick
in two lines across her mouth, put there

by her daughter. Like Gertrude Stein's, her hair
is cut close. Nearby is her wheelchair, painted blue

like a boy's bicycle. It is a weekday in March,
the casino is the size of a hangar that could house

a dozen planes, but it is thousands of machines
that fill the eye, an event of light and color.

The sentences she speaks now are like the sentences
of Gertrude Stein, without the ironies of art.

Her mind is like a compressed accordion, the far
points now near, more present than the present.

Waiting, I am at the food court, reading a magazine
article about the languages the world is losing.

The languages spoken only by a few remaining
people. Or by one remaining person. Or lost

totally, except for the grainy recordings in archives,
mysterious as the sounds made by extinct birds.

The reels on her machine spin, their symbols
never matching. She is playing the one-cent slots,

and her money will go far into the afternoon.
And because waiting is thinking, I am thinking

of the eternity Keats writes about in the sonnet
about the grasshopper and the cricket, *ceasing never*

in the hedges and meadows, in the evening stove:
the grasshopper of summer, the cricket of winter.

THE GALLEONS 1

Her story is a part of something larger, it is a part
of history. No, her story is an illumination

of history, a matchstick lit in the black seam of time.
Or, no, her story is separate

from the whole, as distinct as each person is distinct
from the stream of people that led

to the one and leads past the one. Or, her story
is surrounded by history, the ambient spaciousness

of which she is the momentary foreground.
Maybe history is a net through which

just about everything passes, and the pieces of her
story are particles caught in the interstices.

Or, her story is a contradiction, something ordinary
that has no part in history at all, if history is

about what is included, what is made important.
History is the galleon in the middle

of the Pacific Ocean, in the middle of the sixteenth
century, swaying like a drunk who will take

six months to finally reach his house.
She is on another ship, centuries later, on a journey

eastward that will take weeks across the same ocean.
The war is over, though her husband

is still in his officer's uniform, small but confident
among the tall white officers. Her hair

is marcelled like a movie star's waves,
though she has been too sick with the water's motion

to know that anyone sees her. Her daughter is two,
the blur of need at the center of each day's

incessant rocking. Here is a ship, an ocean.
Here is a figure, her story a few words in the blue void.

UDFJ-39546284

In *bunraku,* when you are watching *bunraku,*
there is that sweet moment in your mind

when you stop noticing the three puppeteers hovering
around each puppet like earnest ghosts

and begin to follow the story being told
by the puppets. The chanter sitting off to the side

voices the love, connivance, outrage,
and eventual reconciliation at the heart of each play,

though often what reconciliation actually meant
was everyone banished, broken, or dead.

The seeing and non-seeing that make humans
humans: I'm thinking now of the placid

English estates where the servants had to face the wall
whenever anyone of importance was near,

where workers had to cut the lawns with scissors
by candlelight at night, to save the master

the trouble of seeing and hearing all that effort.
What the mind does with this kind of information

is probably the knot within the *post-*
in what we call *post-modernism,* knowing all we know

now about the cruelty that made modernism
modernism. In the Philippines, growing up among

servants, I loved the servants the same way
I loved my parents, with helplessness and tyranny.

Walking in the exhibit of the black artist's paintings
of young black men in brocaded tableaus,

I am absorbed by their beauty as much
as I am by finding out that the intricate backgrounds

were outsourced to painters in Beijing, taking part
in the functional ambiguity between

one kind of labor and another. I guess all this matters
only as much as you want it to matter,

the mind making its focal adjustments
between foreground and context, present and past,

as well as it can. For example, this morning
my sister sent me a photograph of my grandmother's

hands. Sitting outside in her wheelchair, taking in
the gold sunshine, my grandmother

had her hands folded in her lap, and I looked at them
until I had to stop. This is foreground.

For context, today I learned that the farthest galaxy
we know of, located by scientists in 2011,

is 100,000,000,000,000,000,000,000 miles away.
It goes by the name of UDFj-39546284,

for reasons that I haven't yet looked up.
In the photograph you can see online, the galaxy looks

like the dusty stuff in the corner of a windowpane,
something you could look at sometimes,

something that is nothing, and has nothing
to do with what you know about distance and time.

THE FLEA

At a certain point I stopped and asked
what poems I could write, which were different

from the poems I wanted to write, with the wanting
being proof that I couldn't write those poems, that they

were impossible. What I could do
was different from what I wanted. To see this

was the beginning of work that could be work,
not simply pursuit after pursuit that was

bound to fail, yearning for qualities that were not mine
and could not be mine. Aiming for a muscular

logic that could be followed by a reader's mind
like an old stone wall running along a landscape, I got

nothing so solid or continuous. The authority
I wanted dissolved always into restlessness,

into a constant gathering of images whose aggregate
seemed like things that had come to settle

inside a glove compartment. I had no faith
in my flaws, but I had a grudging faith

in the particular. There was the actual stone wall,
its mongrel irregular blocks harmonized into use, rich

and ordinary as a soul. There was the flea
that landed on my forearm one night as I sat reading.

The black speck of it, then the outsized sting.
The flea that is an insect, has no wings, can jump

vertically seven inches and horizontally thirteen inches.
The flea that looks, through the magnifier,

like the villain spaceship from a science-fiction movie,
that can live for years in good conditions, and lives

by drinking the blood of animals and birds,
in a practice that is called, by science, hematophagy.

THE GALLEONS 2

Research is mourning, my friend says. Which means what,
exactly, for the things listed in the archives

as filling the galleons when they left Cebu and Manila—
ivory objects, jade objects, copper objects,

brass objects, lacquer objects, mother-of-pearl inlaid furniture,
pearls, rubies, sapphires, bolts of cotton cloth,

silks and gauzes, crepes and velvets, taffetas
and damasks and brocades, stockings, cloaks, robes,

kimonos, bed coverings, tapestries, linens, church
vestments, rugs, blue-and-white porcelain that numbered 1500

in one ship, wax, tallow candles, cordage,
sailcloth, musk, borax, camphor, cigars, varieties of tea,

cinnamon that was dried and powdered, 40,000 pounds of it
listed in one ship's manifest, cloves, pepper,

nutmeg, tamarind, ginger, martaban jars from Burma,
dragon jars from China, Vietnamese jars,

Siamese jars, Spanish jars, 800 jars found with the wreck
of one salvaged ship, jars that would have

contained tar for caulking, oil, wine, bizcocho bread,
salted meats, dried fruits, lard, bacon, beans, chickpeas, lentils,

flour, garlic, cheese, honey, rice, salt,
sugar, food for months, not enough food, not enough water,

chickens, cows, pigs, up to 1000 souls
depending on whether the ship had a tonnage of 300 or 500

or 1000 or 2000, ships that in the 250 years
of the trade route wrecked somewhere along the way

more often than they arrived in Acapulco, sailors,
mercenaries, officers, noblemen and their entourages, priests

and missionaries, slaves that were called *indios*
or *chinos*, nails, tools, iron hoops, fireworks, opals—elegy?

STILL LIFE WITH HELICOPTERS

Almost two thousand years before da Vinci
imagined a machine whose screwlike overhead

motor could lift the machine into vertical flight,
children in China played with bamboo toys

whose propellers, thin and light as dragonfly
wings, were set on a sharpened stick and spun

into the wonder of an object spiraling in the air.
The toys were brought back to Europe by early

travelers, where they gave dreams to certain
men, whose names are now an ornate inventory

on the Wikipedia page: Mikhail Lomonosov,
Christian de Launoy, George Cayley, Alphonse

Pénaud, Gustave de Ponton d'Amécourt, Enrico
Forlanini, Jacques and Louis Bréguet, Jacob

Ellehammer, Emmanuel Dieuaide, Paul Cornu,
and, most dashing of all, Raúl Pateras Pescara

de Castelluccio. Ponton d'Amécourt coined
the term *hélicoptère*, from the Greek words for

helix and *wing*. In time, in no time at all, these
dreamers and their dream-contraptions led to

other dreams, other names: Focke-Wulf, Airbus,
AgustaWestland, Sikorsky Aircraft, Boeing

Vertol, Bell Helicopter, Mitsubishi, Kawasaki,
Fuji Heavy Industries, and dozens of other

manufacturers in the world. There are as many
different kinds of helicopters now as there are

uses for them. In 1974, Aerospatiale, which is
now Airbus, introduced the AS350, also known

as the AStar, a best-selling helicopter offering
high performance, enhanced maneuverability,

and reduced pilot workload. One popular use
of the AStar is *to provide aerial observation*

and support to ground units, which must be
what the Oakland Police Department helicopter

is doing now, while the protesters swarm onto
the 580 Freeway and shut it down, protesting

the grand jury's decision in Ferguson, Missouri,
not to indict the police officer who killed Michael

Brown. The police and news helicopters are
what I hear as I sit at the desk, the desk and its

world of things: the black notebook, the pencils,
the loose change, movie stubs, paper clips,

and fortune cookie slips in a thrift-store saucer,
the green paperweight and the little glass utopia

inside it, the Post-it note listing the plains of
the moon, and the copy of *Brown Girl Dreaming*.

THE GIRL CARRYING A LADDER

On the same day I read about the luxury-goods company
that has produced a punching bag you can buy for $175,000,

I see the photograph of the Palestinian girl who carries a ladder
with her each morning when she goes to school. To scale

the wall of my own understanding of why a punching bag
would cost so much, I have to think about why I'm attracted to

that punching bag the way some people are attracted to pink
kittens or the way some people are attracted to camouflage

or the way some people are attracted to their gods. I want that
punching bag the way the girl carrying the ladder wants to go

to school: relentless, single-minded, and absurd. Carrying
the ladder that is two or three times as tall as she is, leaning

the ladder against the wall that separates her from her school,
the girl goes up the ladder as though it were something she did

every day, which she does. When I think of a punching bag,
I think of sex. When I think of a ladder, I think of picking apples.

When I think of the girl carrying the ladder to go to school,
I think of the neighborhood girls carrying pink camouflage

backpacks, not knowing about the armies that the camouflage
stands for. The logo of the luxury brand is printed all over

the punching bag the way camouflage is all over us: camouflage
bedsheets, camouflage cellphone covers, camouflage shirts

in neon colors that everyone wears, even the people who vote
against guns. We live in paradox and prosper. We live in

paradox and thrive. What I can't figure out is how the girl deals
with the barbed wire at the top of the wall she has to go over.

Or what the ladder weighs. Or what she does with the ladder
when she gets to school. Does she put it against a wall with

the other ladders, the way kids put their bikes in bike racks
at school? What I can't figure out is why two men who look

like gods would want to break down the wall of each other's
faces, knowing there is only blood on the other side. Or why

apples are the fruit children bring their teachers, and why
not coconuts or grapefruit. Or why the neighborhood girls,

on their way to school each morning, carry backpacks that are
so heavy it looks like they are carrying the world on their backs.

THE GALLEONS 3

Because I am one of those people
who will talk to you if you are next to me

on an airplane, I am telling the man beside me
about my life as a teacher and my life

as a poet. He is in his early thirties, served
in the Marine Corps in Afghanistan,

and now works as a long-haul truck driver.
I am going home. He is going home

for a long weekend visit with his parents.
When I ask if he has a wife and kids,

he says that he has his dispatcher.
When I ask about Afghanistan, he says

he has a dog from a shelter named Felix,
who stays with his parents during the weeks

he is away. When I tell him I am trying
to write a poem about the Spanish galleon

trade, he tells me about the things
he carries: hay from Nebraska to Florida,

TVs from Delaware to Mississippi,
bark from California to Texas, refrigerated

foods from Missouri to North Dakota,
rolls of carpet from Alabama to Minnesota,

Victoria's Secret stock from New York
to Arizona, iPhones from Washington

to Iowa, and unspecified hazmat materials
that went with a security escort from Michigan

to Ohio. He has been driving for two years
but eventually wants to get a day-shift

delivery job with FedEx or DHL or UPS.
Close to home and close to my bar, he says.

On the long hauls he listens to audiobooks,
mostly thrillers and fantasy novels, and keeps

track of the number of miles, hoping
to reach a million one day. On his phone

he shows me a photo of Felix: a brown dog
with an old dog's gray muzzle, one eye

softly brown, the other marbled gold
and green, like the weather on another planet.

THE BLINK REFLEX

I have this notion that if you live long enough,
there are three or four great stories that you will have in your life.

A story of a journey or a transformation.
A story of love, which will likely mean the loss of love, a story

of loss. And a story of spiritual illumination,
which, for many, will probably be the moment of death itself,

the story untellable, its beginning and middle
and end collapsing with its teller into a disappearing conclusion.

I have believed long enough in my notion
to know that it is a romantic notion, that it erodes each time

I realize that the shard and not the whole
comprises a life, the image and not the narrative. Otherwise,

there's no reason why all I remember of the airplane
I took as a child from one country to another

is the moist towelette packet we were given with our meal,
the wonder and absurdity of it. Or that, in love,

high in a tree in the dark, and high, he and I sat in the rain-damp
branches and ate 7-Eleven donuts. Or this, this piece

of a story that isn't even mine, that isn't even a story
but a glance of an experience, of the friend who held the stray

dog after it was struck by a car. Not knowing whether the dog
was dead, my friend called a friend

who worked for a vet. Poke the dog in the eye, this friend said.
Because if the animal no longer has a blink reflex,

it probably means the animal is dead. Decades after
college, when you could do such a thing, I typed his name

into a search engine to find out what became of the 18-year-old
boy from the tree. Like dozens of old keys

in a drawer, so many of the wrong people with the right name.
The child dead from leukemia, with a school gym

named for him. The wrestler who had a perfectly square jaw,
like a cartoon police detective in a fedora.

When I arrived at a page that was certainly
about him, I no longer knew the face, but I recognized the life

that he had had. He had transferred to
another college, gone to film school, and become a producer

of TV documentaries. A film about fishermen, the harsh fishing
season in Alaska. A film about Abraham Lincoln

and a film about the last days of Adolf Hitler.
A film about the Sherpas who go up and down the Himalayas.

VIRGINIA WOOLF'S WALKING STICK

Unless you are too sensitive or being affected, you don't cry
over a thing in a museum, knowing what's there

is already dead. But there I was, in grief, because when I bent
to the glass case I saw the walking stick

she left behind on the riverbank before she walked in
and sank and died.

I hadn't known the object would be there,
it was among other objects in an exhibit of writers' artifacts,

a black, sturdy thing that might have been owned
by anyone but was owned by her, the last thing of this world

she touched before she touched the stones
that would go into her pockets, the stones that

were things of another world.
The shock of the walking stick was like and not like

the first time I read something she had written,
when I sat at a library carrel in college, cleared it of the books

someone had left there, and found a volume of her diary
among them. This led to the four other volumes,

then to her actual books. This led to a voice, a way of thought
and being, a way of knowing the ordinary

and the profound, that seemed my voice too,
despite the differences that should have made the affinity

impossible—the years between us, gender and class
and race. But there we were. Looking around

at the things that surround me, I have come to understand
that the test of how well a thing is made

is to look at the places where its parts come together—
joints, seams, corners, folds. I know it's a violence to sense

and sequence, but I'm thinking now about sitting with him
in the car in the hours before dawn,

reading aloud the ugliest parts of Wenderoth's *Letters to Wendy's.*
The parts where the speaker does things to Wendy.

The part where the speaker fucks a Frosty. Back and forth,
by the dim gold light of the car, parked on the street

outside his apartment building, reading, laughing,
breathing. I was in love with him and he was in love

with someone else. This is what we hadn't talked about
all night. Earlier, we had driven to a hill

that looked down on the vast city, lit up
like a circuit board in the overall mechanism of the dark.

We stood, hands in our pockets, shrugging in the summertime
cold of a city by the ocean.

The wind was all the talking there was, and then
we were walking back to the car.

This was some time ago. And I don't seem to understand
any more now than I did then, the hill

continually whirled by the wild air, now empty
of people and incident and time, but still full of original feeling.

DRAGGED MASS

What are we supposed to make
of the granite block dragged across the dirt lot

behind a tractor that has been instructed
to build up a mound out of the displaced dirt, a mess

far away from what we would call the aesthetic
and more to do with the disturbance

of fresh graves or construction, the rock
so enormous it seems more conceptual than actual,

the way large things tend to be, the way scale
is a kind of assertion, the larger

the louder, and the smaller heartbreaking,
so that we want to imagine the theatrics of the dirt lot

back to the artist's hand on paper,
the artist trying to transform desire into vision,

or a representation of something
like vision, one that makes us see the granite

and the hurt earth as images of the body, of gravity,
of what time does to the body,

which is to scour it, which must have something to do
with why I am looking at you now, asleep

among blue sheets as though it is any morning,
in winter light, in the light of the eye.

THE GALLEONS 4

Because I am reading Frank O'Hara
while sitting on a bench at the Brooklyn Promenade

I am aware it is 10:30 in New York
on a Tuesday morning

the way O'Hara was always aware
of what day and hour and season were in front of him

It is 12:20 in New York a Friday
he wrote almost sixty years ago on a July moment

that must have been like the one I am having now
the summer hour blossoming

at the promenades by the rivers and in the parks
and in the quiet aisles of the city

when everyone who should be at work is at work
and the trees are meditating

on how muggy it will be today
and the fleets of strollers are out in the sunshine

expanse of the morning
the strollers that are like galleons

carrying their beautiful gold cargo
being pushed by women whose names once graced

the actual galleons *Rosario*
Margarita Magdalena along with other names

Essie Maja from places that history has patronized
like O'Hara going into the bank

for money or the bookstore to buy
an ugly NEW WORLD WRITING to see what

the poets / in Ghana are doing these days
or the liquor store for liquor

or the tobacconist for tobacco
and sitting at the Brooklyn Promenade I haven't looked

at the news to see who now has died
though my fingers keep touching the phone's face

to find out that when it is 10:30 in the morning
in New York it is 11:30 in the night

in Manila and it is 4:30 in the afternoon in Lagos
and in Warsaw and it is 9:30

in the morning in Guatemala City
where it is also Tuesday and where it is also summer

CASCADES 501

The man sitting behind me
is telling the man sitting next to him about his heart bypass.

Outside the train's window, the landscapes smear by—
the earnest, haphazard distillations of America. The backyards

and back sides of houses. The back lots of shops
and factories. The underpasses of bridges. And then the stretches

of actual land, which is not so much land
as the kinds of water courses and greenery that register

like luck in the mind. Dense walls of trees.
Punky little woods. The living continually outgrowing

the fallen and decaying. The vines and ivies taking over
everything, proving that the force of disorder is also the force

of plenty. Then the eye dilating to the sudden
clearings—fields, meadows. The bogs that must have been left

by retreating glaciers. The creeks, the algae broth
of ponds. Then the broad silver of rivers, shiny

as turnstiles. Attrition, dispersal, growth—a system unfastened
to story, as though the green sight itself

was beyond story, was peacefully beyond any clear meaning.
But why the gust of alertness that comes

to me every time any indication of the human
passes into sight—like a mirror, like to like, even though I am not

the summer backyard with the orange soccer ball resting
there, even though I am not the pickup truck

parked askew in the back lot, its two doors opened
wide, and no one around to show whether it is funny

or an emergency that the truck is like that. Each thing looks new
even when it is old and broken down.

They had to open me up—the man is now telling the other man.
I wasn't there to see it, but they opened me up.

THE MARROW

For a time I lived in a house with a meadow
and small woods around it. It was summer, the light

changing the meadow over the long day,
as though to illustrate the phases of consciousness:

the gold of morning, the stricken green at noon,
the shadows saturated by coolness

in the evening. Butterflies, like small yellow utility
flags, crossed the light. And the sounds

of insects and birds, little strings of notes
on staves. Deer appeared, disclosing this fact:

if you don't have hands, you use your mouth.
Like clockwork, two kept coming back each morning

to the same spots, as though the grass they ate
the day before had sprung back overnight.

They were deer. Because I was not sick or in need,
they were only deer. Behind the glass

of the house, I must have been
a small distortion in the reflection they saw there,

a small motion in the surface. In the woods
were wild roses with pink edges, going white

into their centers. Under the large trees,
the ferns were a dense singularity, the span of each

frond a kind of fractal logic. I saw things
mostly as they were, which meant a kind of health.

The nights were dark, as though the house was far
inland, in the marrow of geography.

But just beyond the house and the meadow
was the ocean, which you could hear if you listened.

We didn't want to be noticed, so we put charcoal on our faces.
I listen to the hours of tape, of the two of us at the dining table.

All the girls, looking like dirt. / My father was always drinking
Questions about the town, her parents, the names of people

or with women, my mother had to take care of the business. /
that only she could now remember. The images, I imagined,

My sister broke her back when she was a child, she grew up
scrolling in her mind, and translated into the answers she gave.

into a hunchback. She died very young. / They set up a dance
Sometimes pausing, not because she couldn't recall, but didn't

at the municipal tennis courts to celebrate the end of the war,
want to recall badly, the pause a kind of gap between what she

and he was there, in his US uniform. / He always insisted that
knew and what the words could do. The two things a voice

we sit at the front, but when I was by myself on the bus I sat
can say when it is saying one thing, the things that suddenly

somewhere in the middle. I didn't want trouble. / I was around
return when you are speaking, like pockets of color coming to

fifty-five when I had my first real job, working as the security
life in your mind: I listen to her with my skin and my eyes,

at Macy's. / I always liked to read. I wanted to go to college
my ears. I had had the notion that asking her about her life

like my sisters, but I got married. / You know that wedding
might add something to what I thought of as my art, as though

dress in the picture, we had to borrow it from our neighbor. /
her past and her love could be vectors of use. But I started to

I liked Japan when he was stationed there. It was so clean.
realize that what I actually needed to know, I would have

Then Norfolk. Richmond. / I was so sick on the ship, I can't
to conjure for myself, because what we know most deeply

remember much. Your mama just kept running all around.
we guard best, even as she spoke, laughed, passed the glow

It was a navy ship. / My mother's name is Canuta Sacay and
of each story to me, like a document I could have in hand

my father's name is Enrique Omega. My grandparents were
but could not understand. I put the tape away, felt for years

farmers outside Ormoc. / I was born in Ormoc, December 8,
that it was enough, the responsibility done. Our conversation

1924 or '25. / This was the apartment we lived in in Maryland.
stopped when my aunt came to take her out for some errands.

That's Junior there in the picture. And there's your mama.
Chatter, chairs moved around, then noises that are just noises.

THE NAMES

Now it's time for the lilac, blazon of spring, the prince
of plants, whose name I know only when it blooms.

The blooms called forth by a bare measure of warmth,
days that are more chill than warm, though the roots must

know, and the leaves, and the spindly trunks ganged up
by the trash bins behind our houses. The blue pointillism

in morning fog. The blue that is lavender. The blue that is
purple. The smell that is the air's sugar, the sweet

weight when you put your face near, the way you would
put it near the side of someone's head. Here the ear.

Here the nape. Here the part of flesh that has no name
at all, the part that is shining because it has slipped naming.

In the crumbling photo album, the dead toddler on a bier,
dead for decades, whose name I now carry. On another

page, the old man, also decades gone, whose same name
I now carry. The name a fossil, the calcium radiance

that I bear and will eventually give up. Again it's time
for the lilacs. The quiet beautiful things at the sides of the

rec center parking lot. The purple surge by the freeway.
The sprigs I cut from the shrub leaning toward me

from the neighbor's yard, taking them at night because
I shouldn't be taking them. The blooms that are a genius

on the kitchen table, awful because I want to eat them
with my terrible eyes, with my terrible hands. The awful

lilacs, the brief lilacs, the sweet. Here is the recklessness
I have wanted. Here is the composure I have earned.

THE GALLEONS 6

Santiago, 1564
San Juan, 1564

San Lucas, 1564
San Pablo, 1564

San Pedro, 1564
San Gerónimo, 1566

San Juan o San Juanillo, 1570
Espíritu Santo, 1570

Santiago, 1572
San Felipe, 1575

Trinidad, 1579
San Martin, 1581

María de Jesús, 1582
San Juan Bautista, 1583

Ntra Sra de Buena Esperanza, 1587
Santa Ana, 1587

Santiago, 1588
San Ildefonso, 1590

San Felipe, 1590
San Francisco, 1593

San Pedro, 1594
Ntra Sra del Rosario, 1594

San Gerónimo, 1595
Santa Margarita, 1595

San Pablo, 1595
San Bartolomé, 1597

San Diego, 1597
La Contadora, 1599

Santo Tomás, 1599
X-M, 1599

X-N, 1599
Ntra Sra del Rosario, 1600

Santa Catalina, 1600
Santiaguillo, 1600

Santa Potenciana, 1600
San Antonio, 1601

Jesús María Joseph, 1601
Ntra Sra de la Antigua, 1602

Ntra Sra de Begoña, 1602
San Francisco, 1602

Espíritu Santo, 1602
San Ildefonso, 1602

Ntra Sra de los Remedios, 1602
San Alfonso, 1603

San Antonio de Padua, 1603
San Diego, 1604

Ntra Sra de la O, 1604
Santa Ana, 1606

San Pedro y San Pablo, 1607
Santiago, 1607

San Andrés, 1609
San Buenaventura, 1609

San Francisco Javier, 1610
San Juan Bautista, 1610

Ntra Sra de Guadalupe, 1612
Santo Ángel de la Guarda, 1612

San Pedro, 1613
Santiago, 1615

San José, 1615
Santa Margarita, 1615

San Antonio, 1615
X-O, 1615

Ntra Sra de los Remedios, 1616
San Gerónimo, 1617

San Marcos, 1617
Espíritu Santo, 1618

San Andrés, 1618
San Juan Bautista, 1618

San Gerónimo, 1619
Jesús María, 1620

Ntra Sra de la Vida, 1621
San Raimundo, 1626

San Juan Bautista, 1629
San Francisco, 1631

Santa María Magdalena, 1631
Ntra Sra de la Encarnación, 1634

Ntra Sra de la Concepción, 1634
San Ambrosio, 1636

San Nicolás, 1636
San Juan Bautista, 1637

San Diego, 1646
Buen Jesús, 1648

Ntra Sra de Guía, 1649
San Juan Evangelista, 1650

San Francisco, 1652
Santiago, 1655

Ntra Sra de la Victoria,1655
San José, 1656

Ntra Sra de la Concepción, 1659
San Damián, 1662

San Sabiniano, 1663
Ntra Sra del Buen Socorro, 1667

San Diego, 1667
Santa Maria de los Valles, 1668

Santo Niño, 1671
San Antonio de Padua, 1672

San Telmo, 1672
Santa Rosa de Lima, 1676

Santo Niño Jesús de Cebú, 1684
Santo Tomas, 1686

Santo Cristo de Burgos, 1688
Santo Rey Don Fernando, 1688

Santa Rosa de Lima, 1689
Ntra Sra del Pilar, 1690

San Felipe, 1690
Ntra Sra del Rosario, 1692

Ntra Sra de la Concepción, 1693
San José, 1694

Ntra Sra de la Concepción, 1694
San José y las Benditas Animas, 1695

San José, 1696
X-T, 1696

Ntra Sra del Rosario, 1703
San Francisco Javier, 1705

Ntra Sra de la Encarnación, 1707
Ntra Sra de Begoña, 1709

Santo Cristo de Burgos, 1713
San Judas Tadeo, 1715

Sacra Familia, 1718
X-U (San Andrés, TA), 1721

Ntra Sra de los Dolores, 1724
Ntra Sra de la Guía, 1728

Ntra Sra de Covadonga, 1731
San Cristobal, 1731

Ntra Sra del Pilar de Zaragoza, 1734
Santa María Magdalena, 1734

Encarnación, 1735
Ntra Sra del Rosario, 1743

San Francisco, 1744
Santo Domingo, 1745

Ntra Sra del Rosario, 1747
Santísima Trinidad, 1751

Ntra Sra del Rosario, 1752
Ntra Sra de la Portería, 1757

Santa Rosa, 1764
Ntra Sra de la Soledad, 1766

San Carlos Borromeo, 1766
San José, 1770

Ntra Sra del Rosario, 1772
Ntra Sra de la Consolación, 1773

Ntra Sra de la Concepción, 1776
San Pedro, 1776

San Antonio, 1779
Ntra Sra del Rosario, 1780

San Andrés, 1784
San Felipe, 1784

Santiago, 1785
Ntra Sra de Asansa, 1785

Felicidad, 1786
San Carlos, 1787

San Andrés, 1787
San José de las Ánimas, 1792

Santa Rosa, 1792
Rey Carlos, 1793

San Fernando, 1794
Concepción, 1795

Ntra Sra de la Santísima Trinidad, 1795
Activo, 1796

Fama, 1798
Ntra Sra del Pilar, 1798

Santa María, 1798
San Cristobal, 1798

San Rafael, 1800
Lucía, 1800

Montañés, 1801
Príncipe de Asturias, 1802

Ntra Sra de la Guía, 1802
Nancy, 1803

Franklin, 1803
Hardinger, 1806

Esperanza, 1806
San Francisco Xavier, 1807

Mosca, 1810
San Antonio, 1813

Fidelidad, 1814
Victoria, 1815

THE GALLEONS 7

We had left the room to make a quiet
for the nurse to wash her in.

To go from us then, to decide,
as in a courtesy. Her soft nod away.

ADJACENT, AGAINST, UPON

I may be looking at the set of boulders
that is now in front of me, but it is you I am addressing.

You are near or you are far,
depending on the accuracy of the words I have chosen.

When my teacher told me to use *this*
instead of *the*, she was talking about the range between

the intimate and the conventional. The gray cluster
is radiant, but it is a melancholy radiance.

To describe it only seems to lean away
from what I intend. Maybe, then, touch is a better way

of explaining the pleasure of that
encounter: the surprise and familiarity of the plant

that you brush past in the dark of your
own house. Or maybe the always-new logic of a dream

is closer to the truth: the falling that takes place
in a place where there is no ground.

The boulders are there for me, an arrangement
and its warren of rooms. One door opening to foggy roses.

Another one opening to a dawn that is the color of tea.
Surely there will always be new language

to tell you who I am, imagination rousing
out of idleness into urgency, reaching now toward you.

I keep remembering my teacher and she is an image
of joy, the small and wordless music

of her silver bangles. *This* over *the*.
One of the rules for writing the poems of a lonely person.

MARIMAR

One of the things I know
is that the most beautiful church in the world

is in the Philippines, in the province of Bohol,
in the town of Baclayon. Built in 1727

by Jesuits who must have believed
its jewel-box interior would subdue the natives

into belief, the church still strikes
each of us, jaded and tired from having seen

too much already, with the solemn hunger
that the place is supposed to stir.

The altar's enormous tableau of saints
is a rococo fantasy now chipping to gold dust,

the walls painted in the pastels
of leaf and shell are now velvety with mildew,

earthquake-cracked into craquelure.
But the floor's patterned marble is still hard

as faith, and the high clerestory stained glass
still filters light in the primary colors

that might organize a city's subway lines:
green, blue, yellow, red. Small in this elaborate

radiance, I think of the poor of the parish,
which would have been the whole

parish, in the candlelight of a dawn mass,
in the light before electricity,

before the end of awe. I think of my own
childhood mornings, serious in altar-boy robes,

the smoke from the censer feathering
into my eyes. And, later, the crooked desires

that would smash the devout in me
to filth. Just down the road from the church,

at the tourist-trap zoo that is really
just someone's grotesque backyard menagerie,

the true attraction is Marimar,
the *Jungle Diva* advertised on the roadside

billboard. In a bustier not meant
to cover her bits of chest hair, a red miniskirt,

and a beehive wig stiff as a top hat,
Marimar guides us past the cages of monkeys,

parrots, and snakes, giving us bright facts,
crisp as a flight attendant announcing

safety information. When one of the pythons
died, Marimar tells us, she turned him

into stew. And I can see it: how Marimar looks
at the world each morning and knows

she was meant to eat all of it. I can see
the life within her mirror as she puts it all on:

the primer, the foundation, the concealer,
the powder, the contouring on nose and jawline,

the highlighting on the cheeks and cupid's
bow, the brow pencil making its

wings, the doe-foot brush of the eyeshadow
applying the light-green shade

that rhymes with the church's crumbling
paint, the long lashes and the Nefertiti eyeliner,

the camellia-red lipstick, the face
that even the strongest key lighting or tropical

heat cannot mar. I'm a good cook, she says,
finishing the joke, flicking open her black lace fan.

WRIGHT PARK

There must be drugs in the backpack
lying on the grass. One cop is leading away

the bicycle, while the other cops stand around
the man handcuffed on the ground,

not moving but clearly not hurt, waiting
like everyone else for what will happen next.

It's just one faggot on a bicycle,
says the old man holding a cane, standing near,

why so many cops? The park is beautiful
at dusk. The sky a blue-gray dome,

the lawns like billiard tables. The hundred
trees exhale a good, cool air.

The statue of Henrik Ibsen looks out over
the pond's mallards, the dog-walkers,

the teenagers smoking on the benches.
I know the mind's violence, and what I see

is an old man in a blue ski jacket
on a summer evening, his cane thin and white

as a toothpick, not stick enough
to beat back the faggots riding into the park

on their bicycles, the faggots in the flower beds,
the faggots in the trees and bushes,

the blue cops who are also faggots,
the faggots splashing into the pond of ducks

and carp, the faggots on the swings,
the faggots, the faggots everywhere, the faggots.

THE GALLEONS 8

The galleons want to go to the opera
because they want to hear emotions as big as their emotions.

When the spurned lover sings
his booming aria, they think of the oceans that cover

the world almost completely.
When the young maid sings her way

to being the queen of a kingdom,
they think of the months-long journeys that will pick off

their crews one by one, in terrifying
weather followed by boredom. And then the galleons want

to shop in the mall in the suburbs.
Everything they see there is like the secrets

they once carried in their holds.
Racks of blouses like sacks of gold, tiers of blenders

like crates of silver. The food courts
remind them of their full bellies before the trips home,

the weight in the center of the body
after it has eaten everything, the stomach glossy and pink

as a shopping bag. And then the galleons
want to visit the boy who loves making model boats

in the basement that his parents have given up
to his hobby. Wearing a magnifying

visor, at a table with glues and tweezers and exact
bits of wood, the boy puts together longships

and carracks in exquisite minute scale.
The galleons approve of the galleon he has been making

for months, imagining the huge tonnage
of the actual ships, their cannons arrayed on the sides

like judges. And then the galleons, on certain
other days, want to go back to the forests

they came from, to reel the blood-soaked narrative
back to the stands of pines and oaks

that will become their keels and decking,
hulls and masts. Back to the mountains being mountains,

their iron in the ground like gray thoughts.
Back to the birds being birds.

Back to the lakes being lakes, deeply shining,
like the black velvet gloves of a prince in an old painting.

ON SOME ITEMS IN THE PAINTING BY VELÁZQUEZ

The LASIK-surgery buzzing that turns out
to be the sound sampled

deep in the electronica track: just so,
the mind can follow

the objects back to their bitter
cartography: the silver tray traced

to the 600 mines and 60 miles of mines
in the mountain in Potosí,

the workers in loincloth and candlelight:
or, on the tray, the red cup

the scholars of material culture
believe to be from Guadalajara,

its clay that gives the water a pleasant
and fragrant flavor: what

the five-year-old infanta must prefer,
though it is not desire

her posture telegraphs, but the self-regard
of someone who understands

she is what economists would call
a positional good: at 21, married

off in Vienna, she will be dead,
her body its own consumed

nexus of labor: several miscarriages, four
children: meanwhile, back in

the immortal childhood, the king
and queen stand in the mirror,

authority and love, the drapery
just behind them a silk fabric dyed

red from cochineal, the natives using
pointed sticks to extract

the dormant bugs from the nopal cactus,
insects as valuable as silver

and gold: each trophy is taken
seemingly for granted, except

the objects are in the central axis
of what Velázquez has organized

in the painting like an exceptional
identity, where we might pause

and see them, or glance past,
these silent detonations the world

has collapsed into: like my own desires,
even though I think

of myself as someone with a regulated
mind, wanting happiness

as simple as a can of yellow paint,
or as perfect as the platinum skull

that my 50 million dollars might
buy, the skull cast by Hirst from

what was once an 18th-century head
and covered with 8,601 diamonds.

THE GALLEONS 9

in Madrid I orient myself   I walk on the wide boulevards
and know an empire is its boulevards   I stand below the angel

skeptical of the beauty of angels   at the royal gardens I count
the 138 kinds of dahlias   at the crystal palace I imagine

the exhibition of plants indigenous to my islands   I walk
up the street of the poets   read the bronze lines on the ground

the longing and song of the pirate   in one museum I stare
at Picasso's lightbulb   in the oldest neighborhoods

I wonder if José Rizal walked these streets   studying diseases
of the eye during the day   writing his novel in the night

in another museum I look   at the paintings of the dwarves
of the horses   of the undying fruit   in the train station

I visit the memorial for the murdered   in the great white
square at dawn I walk   inscribe myself like letters on a page

at the naval museum I look into the face of Magellan   show the
painting my face   I sing the neighborhoods of Huertas

and Chueca   maybe only in Madrid   is the light a gold
weight always   at the supermarket I overhear   two Filipinos

speaking and I turn away and break   I find myself in
the cathedral   in the movie theater   where I watch a movie

without understanding the words spoken   around a corner
I stop because a kind of meadow   has been grown on the side

of a building   like a tallness of heart   a dream carried
into waking   my life breathing before it   incredible and true

BROKEN MIRROR AGAINST TREE TRUNK

The day is strong like a horse swimming across a high river,
or the day is gray, tired, and hoarse.

The tree in its annual nakedness is delicate,
or it is authoritative, like the surgeon in *The Anatomy Lesson*.

Longer than I can remember, I have prayed to the patron saint
of eyesight for a new way, a new accuracy.

The choreographer says that there are no new steps,
only new combinations. So I believe it.

The naturalist says the heart rate of the albatross in flight
is lower than it is at rest. I believe that too.

The artist sews through wood using hair for thread,
at the distal end of an idea we call *patience*.

We get so much winter here. I know it by the mountain held
in its white custody, round as a kneecap.

Or it is that dense silence in the room where a few dozen
people are observing a moment of silence.

Or the neighbors who move and leave things in the yard,
things that are like principles: mop, pennants.

Beauty strides into view all the time, clear and particular
or vague and soft, an affiliation or a polarity.

I have felt squalls in the blood and in the mind,
even though I am mostly like a mirror, its silver blood.

I have been that man in the red baseball cap,
skimming the cruel lawns of the park with his metal detector.

A POEM AS LONG AS CALIFORNIA

This is my pastoral: the used car lot
where someone read "Song of Myself" over the loudspeaker

all that afternoon, to customers who walked among the cars
mostly absent to what they heard,

except for the one or two who looked up
into the air, as though they recognized the reckless phrases

hovering there among the colored streamers,
their faces suddenly loose with a dreamy attention.

This is also my pastoral: once a week,
in the apartment above, the prayer group that would chant

for a sustained hour. I never saw them,
I didn't know the words they sang, but I could feel

my breath running heavy or light
as the hour's abstract narrative unfolded, rising and falling,

sometimes changing in abrupt turns
of speed, as though a new voice had taken the lead.

And this, too, is my pastoral: reading in my car
in the supermarket parking lot, reading the Spicer poem

where he wants to write a poem as long
as California. It was cold in the car, then it was too dark.

Why had I been so forlorn, when there was so much
just beyond, leaning into life? Even the cart

pushed against a concrete island, the forgotten melon
in its basket like a lost green sun.

And this is my pastoral: reading again and again
the paragraph in the novel by DeLillo where the family eats

the take-out fried chicken in their car,
not talking, trading the parts of the meal among themselves

in a primal choreography, a softly single consciousness,
while outside, everything stumbled apart,

the grim world pastoralizing their heavy coats,
the car's windows, their breath and hands, the grease.

If, by pastoral, we mean a kind of peace,
this is my pastoral: walking up Grand Avenue, down Sixth

Avenue, up Charing Cross Road, down Canal,
then up Valencia, all the way back to Agua Dulce Street,

the street of my childhood, terrifying with roaring trucks
and stray dogs, but whose cold sweetness

flowed night and day from the artesian well at the corner,
where the poor got their water. And this is

also my pastoral: in 1502, when Albrecht Dürer painted
the young hare, he painted into its eye

the window of his studio. The hare is the color
of a winter meadow, brown and gold, each strand of fur

like a slip of grass holding an exact amount
of the season's voltage. And the window within the eye,

which you don't see until you see, is white as a winter sky,
though you know it is joy that is held there.

THE GALLEONS 10

I come from the lowlands.
My mother's city was built on the river

where the mountains fanned out to the sea,
and the city thrived there.

I come from farmers.
I come from childhood's transistor radio,

from the kalachuchi tree
and its white flowers. I come from prayer.

My parents took me to a faith healer
once, though no one now recalls

the malady or the terms of the cure.
I had a fate, it took me

across an ocean. It has taken half a life
to turn back and see

what it was I left behind.
I come from teachers and soldiers.

On the island my father comes from,
the people covered their bodies

with tattoos. I come from soot,
from ink. I come from people who honed

their teeth to sharp points,
who buried their dead in coffins

shaped like boats for a journey.
I come from horizon. I come from water.

ODE WITH INTERRUPTIONS

Someone is in the kitchen washing the dishes.
Someone is in the living room watching the news.

Someone in a bedroom is holding a used stamp
with tweezers and adding it to his collection.

Someone is scolding a dog, barking now for
decades, a different dog for each of the decades.

Someone is reading the paper and listening to
a baseball game on the radio at the same time—

At the base of the altar, you drop some coins
into a wooden box and the lights reveal the vast,

worn painting in front of you. The holy subject
is illuminated for a few minutes before it is dim

again. There are churches all over Italy where
you can do this. The smell of incense, stone—

Someone is taking the ashes out of the small
cave of the fireplace, though this might have been

a hundred years ago, when the house was new
and we didn't live in it. Someone is writing

a letter on thin blue paper. Someone is putting
down the needle onto a spinning record, just so.

On the couch, someone is sleeping. Upstairs,
someone is looking into the bathroom mirror—

While we were waiting for her surgery to finish,
I walked around the hospital and came across

a waiting room that had an immense aquarium.
The black fish with red stripes, the yellow fish

with blue stripes, the triangle fish, the cylinder
fish, the little orange schools and the cellophane

glints of their quick turns in the box of water,
among arrangements of coral, the city of bones—

Someone is walking down the creaking staircase
in the dark, a hand sliding on the rail. Someone

is on the telephone, which means nobody else
can use it for another hour. Someone in his room

is doing homework, me or someone almost like
me, twenty, fifty years ago. Someone is reading

in her room. Someone is talking to the gray wall.
Someone is talking to the gray wall. In summer,

on a hot afternoon, someone peels at a corner
of wallpaper and sees more wallpaper beneath—

I used to think that to write poems, to make art,
meant trying to transcend the prosaic elements

of the self, to arrive at some essential plane, where
poems were supposed to succeed. I was wrong.

Acknowledgments

I am grateful to the editors and staff of the following publications, where the poems in this book first appeared: the Academy of American Poets *Poem-a-Day* ("Adjacent, Against, Upon," "Cascades 501," "Dragged Mass," "The Galleons 4"); *Arkansas International* ("Broken Mirror Against Tree Trunk"); *Arroyo Literary Review* ("UDFj-39546284"); *The Awl* ("Virginia Woolf's Walking Stick"); *Bennington Review* ("The Girl Carrying a Ladder"); *Cherry Tree* ("The Names"); *Gulf Coast* ("Wright Park"); *New Republic* ("The Marrow"); *New Yorker* ("The Galleons 8"); *Ploughshares* ("Still Life with Helicopters"); *Poetry* ("The Flea," "The Galleons 1, 2, 5, 9," "Ode with Interruptions"); *San Francisco Chronicle* ("The Galleons 10"); *Seattle Review of Books* ("The Blink Reflex"); *Threepenny Review* ("The Galleons 3," "The Grasshopper and the Cricket"); and *Tin House* ("A Poem as Long as California," "On Some Items in the Painting by Velázquez").

"A Poem as Long as California" and "The Grasshopper and the Cricket" were reprinted on *Poetry Daily*. "The Galleons 10" was reprinted in the *International Examiner*. "Wright Park" was reprinted on *Verse Daily*, *The Rag-Picker's Guide to Poetry* (University of Michigan Press), and *Nepantla: An Anthology of Queer Poets of Color* (Nightboat Books). "UDFj-39546284" was reprinted in *Pushcart Prize XLIII: Best of the Small Presses*.

Acknowledgment is due to the following for their support: the Helen Riaboff Whiteley Center, the John Simon Guggenheim Memorial Foundation, and Pacific Lutheran University. My gratitude to these comrade poets for their invaluable feedback on this book: Oliver de la Paz, Michael Dumanis, Wayne Miller, and Brian Teare.

Rick Barot was born in the Philippines and grew up in the San Francisco Bay Area. He has published three previous volumes of poetry: *The Darker Fall*; *Want*, which was a finalist for the Lambda Literary Award and won the 2009 GrubStreet Book Prize; and *Chord*. *Chord* received the UNT Rilke Prize, the PEN Open Book Award, and the Publishing Triangle's Thom Gunn Award. It was also a finalist for the Los Angeles Times Book Prize. His work has appeared in numerous publications, including *Poetry*, the *New Republic*, *Tin House*, *Kenyon Review*, and the *New Yorker*. He has received fellowships from the National Endowment for the Arts, the Artist Trust of Washington, the John Simon Guggenheim Memorial Foundation, and Stanford University. He is the poetry editor for *New England Review*. He lives in Tacoma, Washington, and directs the Rainier Writing Workshop, the low-residency MFA program in creative writing at Pacific Lutheran University.

milkweed
editions

Founded as a nonprofit organization in 1980,
Milkweed Editions is an independent publisher. Our mission
is to identify, nurture and publish transformative literature,
and build an engaged community around it.

milkweed.org

Interior design by Mary Austin Speaker
Typeset in Columbus
by Rodolfo Avelar

Columbus was designed by Patricia and David Saunders for
Monotype UK in 1992, the quincentenary of Christopher
Columbus's infamous voyage across the Atlantic. The design of
the typeface was inspired by a collection of Virgil's works printed
in 1513 by Jorge Coci, and by Bartolome de Najera's printing of
a writing manual by the Spanish calligrapher Juan de Yciar.